Stitched
for
Fun

Stitched for Fun

35 Easy and Adorable Embroidery Projects

Fiona Goble

Martingale®
& COMPANY

That Patchwork Place® is an imprint of Martingale & Company®.

Martingale & Company
19021 120th Ave. NE, Suite 102
Bothell, WA 98011-9511 USA
www.martingale-pub.com

Mission Statement
Dedicated to providing quality products and service to inspire creativity.

Library of Congress Cataloging-in-Publication Data is available upon request.
ISBN 978-1-60468-141-3

Senior Editor: Lisa John
Photography: Mark Winwood
Production: Laurence Poos
Design: Paul Stradling
Illustrations: Kuo Kang Chen
Publisher: Clare Sayer

16 15 14 13 12 11   8 7 6 5 4 3 2 1

Some of the projects in this book are unsuitable for children under 3 years of age due to small parts. Always keep small or sharp objects (such as needles or buttons) away from small children.

Contents

Introduction

There is something of a buzz in the air about embroidery at the moment. I don't mean everyone's about to start stitching delicate flowers onto linen tablecloths all over again, but people are beginning to want clothes and home accessories that are a bit different. To my way of thinking, there's nothing easier and more enjoyable than customizing a few possessions with some carefully chosen stitches.

You probably know some of the basic stitches already. Even if you don't, I've explained them all here and I'm sure you'll be able to pick them up in no time. You can buy embroidery floss and needles in almost any fabric or craft shop and get going right away. You can transform something ordinary into something special really swiftly – sometimes in just a few minutes.

There are so many things that can be embellished by a bit of embroidery – some items you may already have and some you can make yourself. I've only used a small selection of handmade items here, and I've written some brief instructions on how to make them on pages 104–109.

But you don't have to stop with these. You can make and embroider glasses cases, fabric photo frames, laundry bags, table runners, clothespin bags . . . the possibilities are almost endless.

Sometimes embroidery is about trial and error. And sometimes it's just about what takes your fancy. So browse through the book and have a look through your home and wardrobe and decide where you want to start. Above all, I hope you have fun.

Fiona Goble

The stitcher's kit

One of the best things about the stitching bug is that you only need a few basic pieces of equipment to get started. Better still, all the items are relatively inexpensive. If you don't already have these items in your sewing or craft box, you can easily find them at most craft shops or online craft or fabric stores.

The basics

Embroidery needle
Embroidery needles have sharp points and eyes that are big enough to thread six-strand embroidery floss. A medium-size embroidery needle is suitable for all the projects in this book.

Embroidery floss
I have sewn all the projects in this book with ordinary six-strand embroidery floss (thread) that comes in a rainbow of different colors. The colors you buy will depend on the projects you want to make, but it's a good idea to start out by buying a selection of basic colors that you can then add to. Most embroidery floss sold in craft shops is colorfast but it is worth checking just to make sure. Even if you are embroidering something you don't plan to wash, you will probably still need to spray it with water to remove the marks from your water-soluble pen or quilter's pencil (see "Methods of transferring your pattern," right).

For most of the projects in this book, you will need to use three strands of embroidery floss. In other words, you will need to cut a length of six-strand floss, then divide it in two. In some cases you will need to use fewer or more strands of thread.

Embroidery floss comes in little skeins that are kept together with one or two paper loops. These skeins can easily get tangled, so you might want to take some steps to make sure your threads behave. The easiest way to do this is to wind the whole skein of floss onto a special bobbin that you can buy in craft stores. Alternatively, you could wind the floss around a piece of cardstock with a little slit along one side to hold the end in place.

Fabric
You can embroider almost any fabric. Good fabrics for beginners are medium-weight woven cottons, tightly woven linen and felt. Avoid fabrics that are very stiff, shaggy or very heavily textured. Also avoid fabrics with a very loose weave, since these could pucker easily, and stitches such as French knots (see page 16) could slip through your work and spoil it.

You can embroider stretchy materials such as cotton T-shirts and fleece, although these aren't ideal for beginners because they need a little bit more care.

Methods of transferring your pattern
There are three main methods to transfer your pattern to your fabric:
• A water-soluble pen or quilter's pencil (these work like an ordinary felt tip or pencil but are easily removed with water)
• Dressmaker's carbon paper or transfer paper and an ordinary pencil
• A special transfer pen or pencil, some tracing paper, an ordinary pencil and an iron

For the first two methods you will also need access to a photocopier, a computer with a scanner, or some tracing paper and a black pen.

Each of the three pattern transfer methods will produce a clear outline for you to stitch. For more details about transferring your pattern, see page 17.

Embroidery scissors

These are small, sharp scissors, and I strongly advise you to buy a pair if you do not already have some. Because they are small, they're easier to use than other scissors when snipping thread after you've finished stitching.

The small points are also useful if you need to undo any work. You can use them to pull the thread to undo a few stitches or to snip stitches before pulling them out.

Helpful extras

Trims

For some of the projects you will need trims such as buttons, ribbons, or bias binding. It's a good idea to build up a selection of items like these so you have a choice. The type of trims you choose can make a big difference in the look of your project.

Standard sewing needle

You will need this sort of needle in order to sew any embellishments on to your embroidery, such as the buttons featured in some of the projects.

Embroidery hoops

Embroidery hoops consist of two rings – a smaller fixed ring and an adjustable ring. The idea is that you stretch your fabric across the smaller ring, and then fit it inside the adjustable ring. Hoops are available in a range of sizes and in wood or plastic.

Many people find that hoops make embroidering much easier, but they are not essential, particularly when you are stitching quite sturdy fabrics. Also, you should not use a hoop when embroidering on felt, as it will pull the fabric out of shape.

Thimble

If your fingers become sore from pushing the needle through your fabric, it is worth getting a thimble – though it can take a bit of getting used to.

Stabilizer fabrics

If your fabric is very flimsy or stretchy, you may want to add a stabilizer fabric to the back of it (although I find it perfectly easy to embroider T-shirts without a stabilizer if I stick to a small chain stitch). The most popular stabilizer fabric is an iron-on version that you can tear away from the back of your fabric once your stitching is complete. You can buy this in shops that sell embroidery and sewing supplies, and in online stores.

Iron

You don't have to iron your embroidery projects, particularly if you are embroidering felt or fleece, but an iron is useful for projects you've stitched on crisp cotton or linen. Always press your work on the back and be careful not to press your embroidery work too heavily, as this will make the stitches look flat.

Sew your own

If you're planning to make your own items to embroider you will also need:

Sewing scissors

A good-quality pair of sewing scissors is essential for cutting fabric. Remember to keep them strictly for cutting fabric, as they will quickly become blunt if you use them for cutting paper or cardstock.

Pins

Sharp pins are essential for pinning most of the projects together before you sew. The ones with colored glass heads are useful, as they are less likely to get left in your work by mistake.

Sewing machine

This is optional, as you can sew most of the items in this book by hand. However, a machine will make sewing much quicker and help give you professional-looking results.

Supply of fabrics

The exact fabrics you need depends on what you are making, but a collection of neutral or pastel cottons and linens is a great starting point. Some floral fabrics that you can use to make your own binding will also come in useful (see pages 105 and 108). Remember to preshrink your fabrics by washing them before you unleash your creative talent. Once your work is complete, wash the items by hand in cool water only, just to be on the safe side.

Stitching essentials

There are loads of embroidery stitches, but all the stitches and techniques you need for the projects in this book are illustrated below.

Starting and finishing your work

The easiest way to secure your work at the beginning is simply to tie a knot at the end of your embroidery floss that is large enough not to slip through your fabric. If you prefer not to have knots on the back of your work or are embroidering a particularly fine fabric and using small stitches, leave a 1½"-long (4 cm) tail of floss at the back of your work and simply start stitching. Once you have finished your work, you can weave the tail through the back of your stitches.

Once you've finished, the easiest way to secure your work is to sew a knot at the back.

To do this, take your thread to the back of your work. Pass your needle under the last stitch, then through the loop you have just made. Tighten the knot and snip your thread close to the knot. If you prefer not to have a knot and are using small stitches, you can simply weave the thread through the stitches, and then snip it off.

Stitch library

All the stitches used within this book are explained and illustrated over the next few pages. Most of the stitches are extremely easy and you may be familiar with them already.

Straight stitch
A straight stitch is just a simple single stitch or group of single stitches, like the stitches used to make up a running stitch.

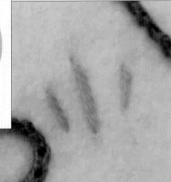

Straight stitch
As used in *The perfect pooch,* pages 54 and 55

11

Star stitch

A star stitch is really a group of straight stitches that are worked across each other to form a star shape.

Star stitch
As used in *Dream a little dream,* pages 38 and 39

Running stitch

For the running stitch, simply insert your needle and take it a stitch width along your fabric and back out again. You can work several running stitches at a time. Running stitches can be worked in different lengths and with different size spaces – but always keep your stitch length and spacing even.

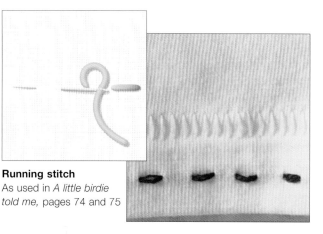

Running stitch
As used in *A little birdie told me,* pages 74 and 75

Threaded running stitch

The threaded running stitch is simply a strand of colored floss sewn along a row of running stitches. Start your second thread at the same point as your running stitches. Simply weave down under the thread of the first running stitch and up under the thread of the second running stitch, without stitching through the fabric, as shown in the photo. You could also weave the thead up over the second stitch, as shown in the illustration.

Threaded running stitch
As used in *Under the sea,* pages 88 and 89

Backstitch

To start, make one forward stitch as if you were working a simple running stitch and bring your needle out to the front of your fabric, a stitch width to the left (1). Then take the needle back into your fabric at the ending point of the stitch you have just made (2) then up through the fabric at 3, a stitch width to the left of the new stitch.

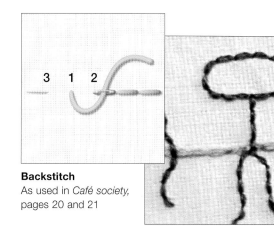

Backstitch
As used in *Café society,*
pages 20 and 21

Stem stitch

Starting at point 1, take your needle to point 2 and then backwards to point 3, which is about halfway between the other two points. You can sew around curves using the stem stitch, but you might need to make your stitches slightly smaller when you do this to make sure the finished curve looks smooth.

When you are using the stem stitch, it is important to always keep your floss on the same side of your needle. If you are sewing a straight line, it doesn't matter which side this is. If you are sewing a curve, keep the floss to the inside of the curve.

To keep your floss neat when working the stem stitch around a corner, take your needle to the back of your work at the corner and tie a knot, as explained in *Starting and finishing your work* on page 11 – but do not trim your thread. Instead, take your needle back out to the front to continue stitching.

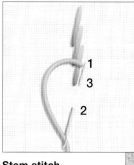

Stem stitch
As used in *Café society,*
pages 20 and 21

Satin stitch

This stitch is used to fill in an area with color with a series of straight lines, as with the boy's cheeks in the example shown. Bring your needle out of your work at 1, back down at 2, out again at 3, down again at 4, out again at 5 and continue in this way until the shape you want to fill is complete. If your shape does not turn out as perfectly even along the sides as you would like, you can work around the sides using a small backstitch.

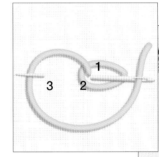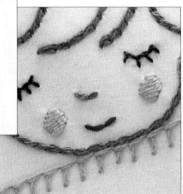

Satin stitch
As used in *Dream a little dream,* pages 38 and 39

Chain stitch

Bring your needle out at the starting point for your stitch (1). Now take your needle back into your fabric, just next to your starting point (2), remembering not to pull the thread too tightly so there is a little loop of thread. Then bring your needle back up through your fabric a stitch width along (3) and catch in the loop. Pull your thread up so it is firm but not too tight.

Chain stitch
As used in *A little birdie told me,* pages 74 and 75

Lazy-daisy stitch

The lazy-daisy stitch is really a group of single chain stitches, all starting around a single point. To make the first stitch, make a single chain stitch as described above. Secure the loop to the fabric with a small stitch, and then take your needle to the starting point of the next stitch.

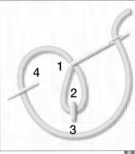

Lazy-daisy stitch
As used in *Elephants on parade,* pages 70 and 71

Scallop stitch

This stitch is a bit like working a lazy-daisy stitch where the beginning and end of the chain stitch are not so close together. Scallop stitches are usually worked as a series. You can make the stitches fairly wide or much narrower, as shown here. From your starting point (1), take your needle down through your fabric (2) leaving a little loop of thread. Bring your needle out of your fabric again where you want your stitch to end (3) and pass your needle under the loop of thread. Pull your stitch fairly taut. Secure the loop by taking your needle down through your fabric, just to the outer side of the loop (4). Bring the needle out again at 2 to start the next stitch.

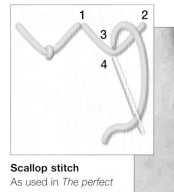

Scallop stitch
As used in *The perfect pooch,* pages 54 and 55

Blanket stitch

To start, bring your needle out on the line or edge that you are embroidering (1). Take the needle down through your fabric a stitch length and a stitch width to the right (2). Bring your needle up on the line, immediately below where you have taken it down (3), making sure you have caught the thread under the needle tip. Pull the thread fairly tightly.

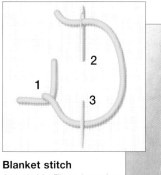

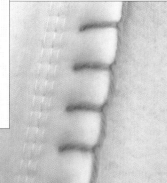

Blanket stitch
As used in *Three beasties,* pages 66 and 67

French knot

To make a French knot, it's easier to work with a fairly short length of thread and to make the stitch close to your fabric. First, bring your thread up at your starting point and wind the thread twice around the needle (1). (Some of the projects in this book involve winding the thread around just once and if this is the case I'll mention it in the instructions.)

Holding the thread taut, take the tip of your needle back into your fabric, just to the side of your starting point (2). It is important you don't take your needle back into the exact starting point or your knot will slip through your fabric! Continue pulling your needle through your work and slide the knot off the needle and onto your fabric. Either tie a knot beneath the fabric to hold the French knot in place or take it back to the front ready to work the next stitch.

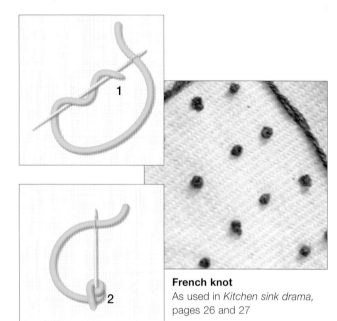

French knot
As used in *Kitchen sink drama,* pages 26 and 27

Sorting out tangles and knots

Sometimes when you're stitching, your floss may appear to have developed a knot. This is usually because it has become twisted. You can undo it by pulling the thread gently on either side of the "knot."

At other times the strands of the floss might look a bit uneven or tangled. To sort this out, run your fingers along the length of the thread to smooth it out.

Knot-free stitching ahoy
Sail away with me, pages 92 and 93

How to use the patterns

There are a number of ways to transfer the patterns in this book onto your fabric. The method you choose partly depends on your own preference. It will also depend on the type of fabric you are using and whether you are embroidering a simple piece of fabric or a ready-made item. Remember that the patterns are all shown at the actual size they have been used in the projects photographed. You can make the patterns smaller or larger to suit your particular project, either on a photocopier or by scanning it into a computer. But remember, some patterns might not work as well if they are made very big and if you make them too small, some of the patterns will be tricky to stitch.

Method 1

Tracing directly onto your fabric

If you are using a fairly thin fabric, you can trace the design directly onto the fabric.

You will need access to a photocopier, a computer with a scanner or some tracing paper and a black pen. You will also need a water-soluble pen or quilter's pencil.

Either photocopy, scan and print or trace the pattern. Then tape the pattern onto a sunny window and trace it directly onto your fabric using a water-soluble pen or quilter's pencil.

If you own a light box (a box with a light inside and a translucent white glass or plastic cover) or are prepared to invest in one, this will save you relying on the weather or time of day!

Method 2

Using dressmaker's carbon paper or transfer paper

You can use this method to transfer your design onto any weight of fabric.

You will need access to a photocopier, a computer with a scanner or some tracing paper and a black pen. You will also need a piece of dressmaker's carbon paper or transfer paper, in a color that will show up on your fabric, and an ordinary pencil.

Either photocopy, scan and print or trace the pattern. Lay the carbon or transfer paper face down on your fabric. Then place the pattern on top of the paper and trace around it with a pencil. When you lift the carbon or transfer paper away, the design will have been transferred to the fabric.

Method 3

Using a transfer pen or pencil

First trace the image onto tracing paper using an ordinary pencil. Then turn the paper over and trace over the lines your have already made using a transfer pen or pencil. Tape the paper, transfer side down, and transfer with an iron, following the instructions that come with the transfer pen or pencil.

Note

All the measurements in this book are given in imperial units (inches or fractions of an inch) with the metric units given in parentheses afterward. Because it is difficult to convert small units of measurement exactly, it is important that you use one system or the other, rather than a mix of the two.

Eat

1

Café society

Who can resist popping in for coffee at a traditional street café in Paris? The smell of freshly made coffee, the delicious pastries, the dapper waiters – and even the lively accordion music. Now you can create your own French café anywhere you like. I made this apron using a vintage apron pattern, but you could easily use a ready-made apron or a modern pattern. Surf the Web for some ideas and free patterns.

Get stitching ...

Transfer the pattern on page 110 onto your apron pocket or pocket fabric.

Work around the top and sides of the roof canopy in chain stitch using three strands of bright red embroidery floss. With the same floss, work the stripes and lower edge in backstitch and a row of scallop stitches along the lower edge.

Work around the plant in chain stitch using three strands of leaf green embroidery floss. Work the stem and branches in backstitch using three strands of dark brown embroidery floss. Work the plant pot in chain stitch using three strands of terracotta floss.

Work the outline of the building in stem stitch using three strands of caramel floss.

Work the table and chairs in backstitch using three strands of dark gray floss.

Work the café door in stem stitch using three strands of mint green floss. Using the same floss, work the door panels in running stitch. Use the same color again for the two lazy-daisy stitches and French knot. Work a single French knot for the doorknob using six strands of dark gray floss.

You will need

X Embroidery floss (thread) in the following colors:
  Bright red for the canopy
  Royal blue for the shutters
  Pale gray for the windows
  Mint green for the door
  Caramel for the building
  Dark gray for the table, chairs and doorknob
  Leaf green for the plant
  Dark brown for the plant stem and branches
  Terracotta for the plant pot

X Embroidery needle

X Embroidery scissors

X Piece of medium-weight white fabric for the pocket, approximately 8" x 10" (20 x 25 cm)

X Ready-made or handmade apron

X 20" (50-cm) length of white lace for the pocket edging (optional)

X Sewing thread to match your pocket fabric

X Sewing scissors

X Standard sewing needle or sewing machine

X Iron

Stitches used

Straight stitch, running stitch, backstitch, stem stitch, chain stitch, lazy-daisy stitch, scallop stitch, French knot

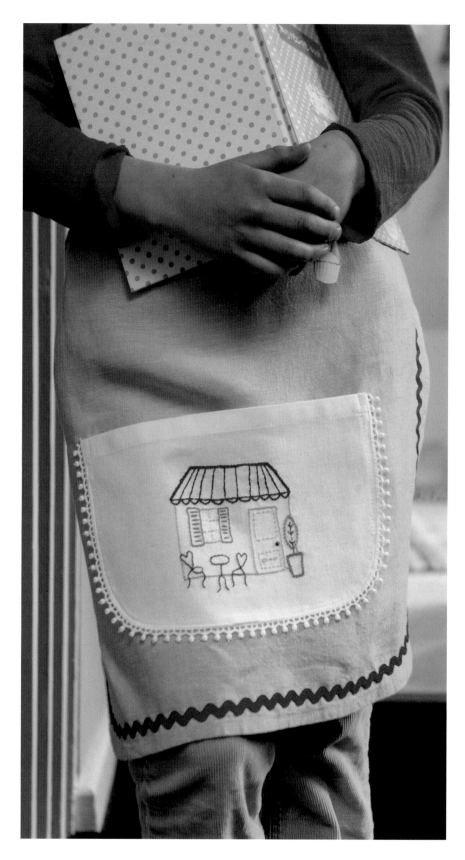

 Work the shutters in backstitch and the shutter louvers in straight stitch using three strands of royal blue floss. Work the top and bottom of the window in backstitch using three strands of pale gray floss. Work the windowpanes in running stitch using the same floss.

 Before stitching the pocket in place, I rounded the lower corners, made a double hem at the top and pressed under the raw edges. I also added some white lace around the edge.

stitch it!

This design would also look great on a plain tea towel, as a small picture for a kitchen or dining room or on a cushion with a lace border.

A nice cup of tea

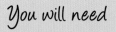

Whatever the weather and whatever the time of day, there's nothing more refreshing than a nice cup of tea. And it has to be in one of my favorite spotty cups, immortalized here. I made the place mats from scraps of fabric in my stash. You could easily buy fabric mats to embroider, but if you want to make your own, turn to page 104.

Get stitching . . .

Transfer the teacup and saucer pattern on page 110 onto the center of your place mat. If you are making your own mats, transfer the pattern onto the center of the central fabric panel before you sew the mat pieces together.

Work the outline of the main part of the cup and saucer in chain stitch using three strands of royal blue or red embroidery floss. Using the same floss, work the handle in stem stitch and the inner ring of the saucer in running stitch.

Work the spots in chain stitch using three strands of pale blue floss on the royal blue cup and three strands of lime green floss on the red cup.

If you are making your own place mats, sew the pieces together, referring to page 104 as needed.

stitch it!

This design would also look great on the corner of large linen napkins, on a striped tea towel or on a greeting card for a friend.

Let them eat cake

When you need a little afternoon pick-me-up, nothing fits the bill quite so well as a delicious cupcake. The sensation of sinking your teeth through the swirl of icing and soft spongy cake is hard to beat. So why not embroider these napkins to accompany your teatime treat? I used large linen napkins for this project and dyed them pink. If you want to make your own napkins, simply double hem a 20" (50 cm) square of linen or cotton fabric.

Get stitching . . .

Transfer the cupcake pattern on page 111 onto the corner of your napkin.

Work the icing on top of the cupcakes in chain stitch using three strands of bright pink or bright yellow embroidery floss.

Work the cake tops of the cupcake in stem stitch using three strands of pale beige embroidery floss.

Work the outline of the cupcake liners in chain stitch using three strands of lime green or turquoise floss. Work the vertical lines on the cases in backstitch using the same floss.

Work a line of large running stitches around the border of the napkins using three strands of deep yellow or red embroidery floss.

Sew the buttons in place on top of the icing, as shown in the picture.

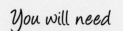
You will need

X Embroidery floss (thread) in the following colors:
Turquoise and lime green for the cupcake liners
Pale beige for the cake tops
Bright yellow and bright pink for the icing
Red and deep yellow for the napkin borders

X Embroidery needle

X Embroidery scissors

X Ready-made or handmade napkins

X Red button and green button for the cake decorations

X Sewing needle and thread to sew on the buttons

Stitches used

Running stitch, backstitch, stem stitch, chain stitch

stitch it!

This design would look great on a greeting card, a table runner or a fabric doorstop for the kitchen.

Kitchen sink drama

You will need

X Embroidery floss (thread) in the following colors:
Turquoise for the whisk handle
Dark gray for the whisk
Crimson for the slotted spoon handle
Purple for the slotted spoon
Leaf green for the serving fork
X Embroidery needle
X Embroidery scissors
X Tea towel

Stitches used

Running stitch, backstitch, stem stitch, French knot

Sometimes you've just got to embrace those domestic chores that could easily get you down – so add a bit of cheer to your kitchen towels with these brightly embroidered cooking utensils. Plain or simple striped tea towels work best for this project.

Get stitching . . .

Transfer the kitchen utensils pattern on page 111 onto the corner of your tea towel.

Work the whisk handle in stem stitch using three strands of turquoise embroidery floss. Work the whisk in running stitch using three strands of dark gray floss.

Work the handle of the slotted spoon in stem stitch using three strands of crimson floss. Work the hole in the handle in backstitch using the same floss. Work the outline of the slotted spoon in stem stitch using three strands of purple floss. Using the same floss, work French knots to represent the spoon holes.

Work the outline of the serving fork in backstitch using three strands of leaf green embroidery floss. Using the same floss, work the hole in backstitch.

stitch it!

This motif would also look great on a fabric serving mat, a curtain for a kitchen, or an apron.

Sweetest little baby face

What self-respecting little angel wants a dreary plain bib when she could cheer up mealtimes in a bib like this? It's never too early to make your mark in the world of fashion. I used a ready-made bib, but you could easily make your own. Surf the Web for a pattern to download or make your own pattern from an existing bib.

Get stitching ...

- Transfer the pattern on page 112 onto your bib.

- Work around the outline of the baby's face in stem stitch using three strands of pink-colored embroidery floss. Using the same floss, work three tiny backstitches for the nose. Again using the same color, work around the baby's hands in backstitch.

- Work around the shirt in stem stitch using three strands of turquoise embroidery floss.

- Work around the hair in backstitch using three strands of ginger brown embroidery floss.

- Work French knots for the eyes using three strands of dark gray floss. Make three straight stitches using two strands of the same color for the eyelashes.

- Work the mouth in backstitch using three strands of red embroidery floss.

- Embroider the cheeks in satin stitch using three strands of pale pink embroidery floss. If you need to neaten the edges of the satin stitch, work a ring of small backstitches.

- Work around the spoon in backstitch using three strands of red embroidery floss. Then work tiny running stitches around the center of the spoon.

- Working in backstitch with three strands of floss, complete the bowl in lime green, the bottle top in purple and the bottle itself in royal blue. Using the same floss, add a few small straight stitches to the side of the bottle to indicate the measuring lines.

- Work the tabletop in chain stitch using three strands of purple floss.

- Sew the little bow just below the neckline of the baby's shirt.

You will need

- ✗ Embroidery floss (thread) in the following colors:
  Pink for the baby's head, nose and hands
  Pale pink for the cheeks
  Ginger brown for the hair
  Turquoise for the baby's shirt
  Purple for the table and bottle top
  Royal blue for the bottle
  Lime green for the bowl
  Red for the mouth and spoon
  Dark gray for the eyes and eyelashes

- ✗ Sewing needle

- ✗ Embroidery needle

- ✗ Embroidery scissors

- ✗ Woven cotton baby bib

- ✗ Small ready-made bow in pale turquoise – or a small length of narrow ribbon to make a bow yourself – and some matching thread to sew it on

Stitches used

Straight stitch, running stitch, backstitch, stem stitch, satin stitch, chain stitch, French knot

---

stitch it!

This motif would look great on a card to celebrate the birth of a baby, on a fabric cover for a photo album or on a baby's T-shirt.

Do the funky chicken

stitch it!

This motif is also great on a simple felt egg cozy, a fabric pot holder or a set of Easter place mats.

Chickens have always been popular in the kitchen. Chicken lovers can buy chicken-shaped chopping boards, kitchen timers, cookie cutters . . . you name it. So why not create your own chicken cup cozy to keep your coffee piping hot?

Get stitching . . .

Cut your cozy shape from the felt. Wrap the piece of felt around the cup. With a water-soluble pen or quilter's pencil, draw a line toward the top of the felt and a lower line, so the two lines are about 2¾" (7 cm) apart. Cut along these lines. Finally, trim the side edges of the cozy so they are vertical and overlap by about ⅜" (1 cm) at the back of the cup.

Transfer the pattern on page 112 onto the center of the cozy.

Work the chicken outline in stem stitch using three strands of purple embroidery floss. Using the same floss, work the wing in backstitch. Work three lazy-daisy stitches for the tail, again using the same floss.

Work the breast in small running stitches using three strands of bright pink floss.

Work a French knot for the eye using three strands of dark gray floss. Work straight stitches around the eye using two strands of turquoise floss.

Work the legs in backstitch using three strands of orange embroidery floss. Add the feet in straight stitch.

Work two straight stitches for the beak using six strands of orange floss.

Work the grass in straight stitches using three strands of leaf green floss.

Add a running-stitch border around the entire cozy using six strands of crimson embroidery floss. Fasten the cozy at the back by overlapping the side edges and stitching or gluing them together.

Sleep

2

The cat's whiskers

In my next life, I'm definitely coming back as a cat so I can stretch out in the sunshine, have someone to wait on me and generally laze about. What could be more perfect? These pajamas were made from an inexpensive pattern I downloaded from a website – but you could just as easily embroider a pair of ready-made pajamas or other garment.

Get stitching ...

- Transfer the cat pattern on page 113 onto the pocket of the pajama top.

- Work the entire outline of the cat in stem stitch using three strands of pale gray embroidery floss.

- Work the cat's stripes in chain stitch using three strands of terracotta embroidery floss.

- Work the eyes and whiskers in backstitch using two strands of dark gray floss.

- Work the nose in satin stitch using three strands of dark gray floss, adding a vertical straight stitch at the base.

You will need

- X Embroidery floss (thread) in the following colors:
  Pale gray for the outline of the cat
  Terracotta for the stripes
  Dark gray for the eyes, nose and whiskers
- X Embroidery needle
- X Embroidery scissors
- X A pair of child's pajamas

Stitches used

Straight stitch, backstitch, stem stitch, satin stitch, chain stitch

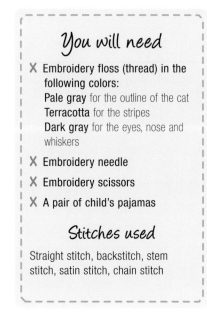

stitch it!

Try this design on a greeting card for a feline lover, on a fabric bag or on a sweet little cushion.

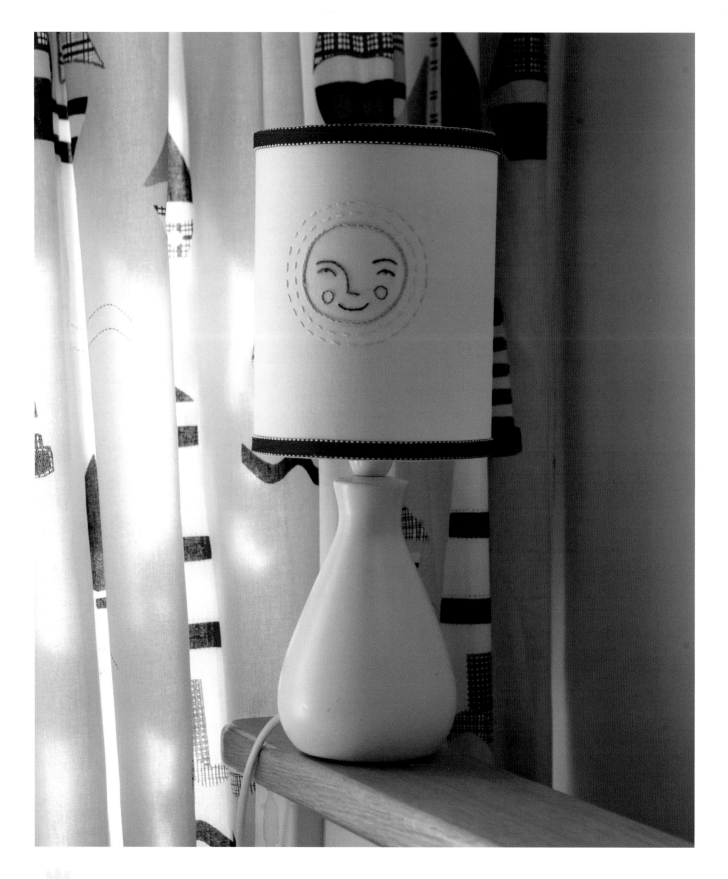

Give me the moonlight

If you've lived with the minimalist look for too long and want to bring a bit of fun into your bedroom, why not embroider your own moonlight lampshade? The embroidered moon and the bright velvet ribbon around the edges are the perfect way to perk up an inexpensive bedside lamp.

You will need

X Embroidery floss (thread) in the following colors:
   Deep yellow for the moon face
   Bright yellow for the inner ring
   Pale pink for the outer ring
   Dark gray for the eyes, eyebrows and nose
   Dusky pink for the cheeks
   Crimson for the mouth

X Embroidery needle

X Embroidery scissors

X A ready-made ivory fabric lampshade or a piece of ivory fabric to cover a lampshade

X Velvet ribbon to go around the top and bottom of your lampshade

X Fabric glue

Stitches used

Running stitch, backstitch, stem stitch, chain stitch, French knot

stitch it!

This motif looks great on a fabric doorstop for your bedroom, as a simple framed picture or on a simple drawstring bag to hold jewelry or special treasures.

Get stitching . . .

Transfer the moon pattern on page 113 onto the center of your ivory lampshade. Alternatively, you could transfer the pattern to a piece of plain ivory fabric, which you can then use to cover your lampshade. If your lampshade has a plastic backing, it is a good idea to prick it with your needle before you make your stitches, as this will make it much easier to stitch.

Work around the outline of the moon in chain stitch using three strands of deep yellow embroidery floss.

Work the nose, eyebrows and upper part of the eyes in stem stitch using three strands of dark gray floss. Using the same floss, work French knots for the eye centers.

Work the outline of the cheeks in backstitch using three strands of dusky pink embroidery floss.

Work the mouth in backstitch using three strands of crimson embroidery floss.

Work the inner circle around the moon in running stitch using three strands of bright yellow floss.

Work the outer circle in running stitch, using three strands of pale pink floss.

Using fabric glue, attach the ribbon around the top and bottom of the shade.

Dream a little dream

Most parents agree that their little angels look at their absolute sweetest tucked in bed. This motif is the perfect adornment for children's bed linen – if only to encourage them to close their eyes and fall asleep. I've used a ready-made crib-sized pillowcase with a drawn threadwork border but it would work just as well on a standard-sized pillowcase.

Get stitching ...

• Transfer the pattern of the sleeping child on page 112 onto the corner of your pillowcase.

• Work the face outline in stem stitch using three strands of dusky pink embroidery floss. Using the same floss, work the nose and hands in backstitch.

• Work the cheeks in satin stitch using three strands of pale pink embroidery floss.

• Work the hair in stem stitch using three strands of medium-brown floss.

• Work the eyes in backstitch using two strands of dark gray embroidery floss. Using the same color, work the lashes in straight stitch.

• Work the mouth in backstitch using three strands of dark pink embroidery floss.

• Work the blanket in blanket stitch using three strands of lime green floss.

• Work the moon in bright yellow backstitch and the stars in deep yellow star stitch.

You will need

X Embroidery floss (thread) in the following colors:
Dusky pink for the face, hands and nose
Pale pink for the cheeks
Dark pink for the mouth
Medium brown for the hair
Bright yellow for the moon
Deep yellow for the stars
Dark gray for the eyes and lashes
Lime green for the blanket
X Embroidery needle
X Embroidery scissors
X Small pillowcase

Stitches used

Straight stitch, star stitch, backstitch, stem stitch, satin stitch, blanket stitch

stitch it!

This motif is also great on a child's dressing gown, a cozy fleece blanket or a plain woolen cushion on a bedroom chair.

! Please note that pillows are not suitable for children under the age of 12 months because of the risks of overheating and suffocation.

Bunny hugs

stitch it!

This design is also perfect for a baby's sleep suit or a baby's hat. You could string a group of bunnies together to make a decoration or mobile.

Rabbits are about the cutest animals ever with their fluffy coats and twitchy noses – until, of course, they munch their way through the prized lettuces in your vegetable patch. Thankfully, when these little embroidered creatures have finished playing outside, they're ready to go upstairs to bed.

Get stitching . . .

Transfer the bunny patterns from page 113 onto your felt.

Work the outline in chain stitch using three strands of bright pink or medium blue embroidery floss.

Work the outline of the dresses in chain stitch using three strands of either turquoise or deep pink embroidery floss.

Work the stripes of the dresses in running stitch using three strands of lime or leaf green floss.

Work the flower petals in lazy-daisy stitch using three strands of turquoise or deep pink floss. Work French knots for the flower centers using three strands of either lime green or deep yellow floss.

Work French knots for the eyes using four strands of dark gray embroidery floss. Using the same floss, work a simple cross for the nose and mouth.

To make the bunny embroidery into a stuffed creature, place it right side up on a piece of matching felt. Work a row of small running stitches around the edge, leaving an opening down the right-hand side of the dress. Trim close to the edge, taking care not to cut through the stitching. Stuff the bunnies lightly and continue your running stitch to close the gap.

Work

3

Home sweet home

One of my favorite childhood images is of fairies' and elves' toadstool cottages. They seemed so perfect with their tiny windows and front doors, and I could imagine all manner of miniature accessories inside. This toadstool cottage embroidered on felt has been used to jazz up a plain, inexpensive address book bought from a stationery store.

Get stitching ...

Transfer the toadstool pattern from page 114 onto your piece of cream felt.

Work the outline of the toadstool roof in chain stitch using three strands of red embroidery floss. Work the spots in chain stitch using three strands of pale blue floss.

Work the sides of the toadstool in stem stitch using three strands of pale brown embroidery floss.

Work the window in backstitch using three strands of turquoise embroidery floss.

Work the outline of the door in chain stitch using two strands of orange floss. Work the door planks in running stitch using the same floss. Work a French knot for the doorknob using three strands of dark gray floss.

Work the flowers in lazy-daisy stitch using three strands of bright pink embroidery floss. Work French knots for the centers using three strands of bright yellow embroidery floss, remembering to wind your thread just once around the needle instead of the normal twice.

Work the flower stems in backstitch using two strands of leaf green embroidery floss. Using the same thread work lazy-daisy stitches for the leaves.

You will need

X Embroidery floss (thread) in the following colors:
Red for the toadstool top and border of the book's spine
Pale blue for the spots
Pale brown for the toadstool stalk
Turquoise for the window
Orange for the door
Dark gray for the door knob
Bright pink for the flowers
Bright yellow for the flower centers
Leaf green for the flower stems and leaves
Lime green for the grass
Cream for the borders

X Embroidery needle

X Embroidery scissors

X A piece of cream felt measuring 4" x 4¾" (10 x 12 cm), rounded at the corners

X Two 9" (23 cm) squares of lime green felt

X A piece of gray felt for the spine

X A hardback address book (approx 6" x 8¼"/15 x 21 cm)

X Fabric glue

X Sewing scissors

Stitches used

Straight stitch, running stitch, backstitch, stem stitch, chain stitch, lazy-daisy stitch, blanket stitch, French knot

Work the grass in lime green straight stitch.

Trim the lime green felt squares so they are just slightly larger than the cover of your book. The gray felt for the spine should be the same length as the lime green squares and about 2" (5 cm) wide.

Work a row of running stitches around the top and outer edge of both pieces of lime green felt using three strands of cream embroidery floss. Work a row of running stitches down both sides of the gray felt spine using three strands of red floss.

Fasten the toadstool embroidery to one of the pieces of lime green felt with blanket stitch using three strands of cream floss.

Using fabric glue, stick the covers and spine in place on the address book.

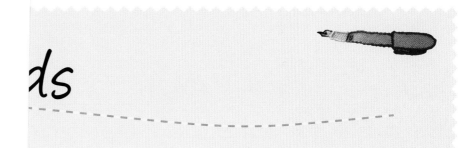

ds

s of people are fed up with emails these days, and I'm
dicting that old-fashioned letter writing will stage a comeback.
here's an embroidered pen for you to stamp your mark on your
ncil case – and other items too, of course. I made this simple
ncil case from two small pieces of faded denim and a zipper, but
could just as easily use a plain ready-made fabric pencil case.

t stitching ...

Transfer the pen pattern on page 114 onto the pencil case or the ric that you are using.

Work the pen outline in stem stitch using three strands of deep pink broidery floss. Using the same floss, d two straight stitches at the base he barrel; then, using six strands of same color, work the clip in chain ch.

Work the grip section of the pen in stem stitch using three strands of e green embroidery floss.

Work the nib in backstitch using three strands of black embroidery floss. Add a straight stitch and French knot at the center.

Work the squiggle in running stitch using three strands of turquoise embroidery floss.

stitch it!

*This motif is also suitable for
a bookmark, a fabric school bag
or a journal cover.*

Wise old owl

Owls have always been considered clever birds, which makes this wise old bird the ideal decoration for your book bag. You could sew the owl onto a ready-made bag, but if you want something a little different, like the bag shown here, see page 105 for some simple instructions. If you are making your own bag, embroider the front piece of the bag before you sew the bag together.

Get stitching ...

- Transfer the owl pattern on page 115 onto your bag or fabric.

- Outline the body in chain stitch using three strands of crimson embroidery floss.

- Work the outline of the top of the head and wings in chain stitch using three strands of purple embroidery floss.

- Work the outer eyes in chain stitch using three strands of leaf green embroidery floss. Make a French knot for the center of the eyes using three strands of dark brown floss. Using the same floss, make a ring of small straight stitches on the inside of the outer eyes.

- Outline the breast in chain stitch using three strands of pale orange embroidery floss. Work the lines across the breast in running stitch using three strands of lime green floss.

- Work the beak in satin stitch using three strands of bright orange embroidery floss, adding a couple of backstitches along the sides of the beak.

- Work the branch in stem stitch using three strands of medium brown embroidery floss.

- Make the legs and claws in stem stitch using three strands of pale orange embroidery floss.

- Work the outline of the leaves in stem stitch using three strands of medium green embroidery floss. Using the same floss, work the center vein of the leaves in running stitch.

- If you are making your own bag, sew the bag pieces together now, referring to page 105 as needed.

see page 105 for some simple instructions

You will need

X Embroidery floss (thread) in the following colors:
  Crimson for the body outline
  Purple for the top of the head and wings
  Leaf green for the outer eyes
  Dark brown for the eye centers and small eye lines
  Pale orange for the breast outline, legs and claws
  Lime green for the lines across the breast
  Bright orange for the beak
  Medium green for the leaves
  Medium brown for the branch

X Embroidery needle

X Embroidery scissors

X A ready-made cotton bag or, if you want to make your own bag, fabrics, matching threads, a sewing machine, sewing scissors and an iron

Stitches used

Straight stitch, running stitch, backstitch, stem stitch, satin stitch, chain stitch, French knot

stitch it!

This design looks great as a picture for your study wall, on a fleece throw for a playroom or den or made into a small felt or cotton toy.

48

Ring my bell

You will need

- X Embroidery floss (thread) in the following colors:
  Red for the outline of the phone and receiver
  Dark gray for the dial and cord
  Bright yellow for the finger holes on the dial
- X Embroidery needle
- X Embroidery scissors
- X A 9" (23 cm) square of green felt
- X Matching thread for the felt
- X A snap fastener
- X A contrasting button
- X Standard sewing needle or sewing machine
- X Sewing scissors

Stitches used

Running stitch, backstitch, stem stitch, French knot

stitch it!

This design looks great on the cover of a small book where you keep your phone numbers, on a fabric doorstop for your study or office or on a felt wall pocket.

Even those who remain skeptical about the benefits of modern technology agree that mobile phones have become one of life's essentials. If, like me, you can never find the sleek black phone lurking at the bottom of your handbag, it's time to make it a bright new home.

Get stitching ...

Using your phone as a guide, cut two pieces of felt to make your phone case, plus two pieces approximately 2½" x 1¼" (6 x 3 cm) for a fastening strap at the top.

Transfer the phone pattern on page 115 onto one of the felt pieces.

Work the receiver and majority of the outline of the phone in stem stitch using three strands of red embroidery floss. Work the two prongs at the top of the phone in backstitch using the same floss. Work the horizontal line below the dial in backstitch, again using the same floss.

Outline the dial in backstitch using three strands of dark gray embroidery floss. Work a French knot at the center of the dial using the same floss. Make French knots to represent the holes in the dial using three strands of bright yellow floss.

Work the cord in running stitch using three strands of dark gray embroidery floss.

Using running sitch, sew the front and back pieces of the phone case together by hand or with a machine and run a line of stitching around the top.

Fasten the two strap pieces together in the same way and fasten the strap to the inside of the back of the case. Sew the button to the front of the strap and add a snap fastener under the button and in a corresponding place on the front of the case.

Relax

4

The perfect pooch

Do you love the idea of owning a dog but are put off by the commitment and the worry of inclement weather? This embroidered picture will help you enjoy some benefits of dog ownership without the hassle. The picture is embroidered on cream felt and displayed in a hand-painted and distressed frame.

Get stitching ...

🔘 Transfer the pattern on page 117 onto your piece of felt.

🔘 Outline the man's face in stem stitch using two strands of pink embroidery floss. Using the same floss, work the hands in scallop stitch and a small straight stitch for the nose.

🔘 Work the hair in backstitch using three strands of ginger brown embroidery floss.

🔘 Work the mouth in backstitch using three strands of deep pink embroidery floss.

🔘 Make two French knots for the man's eyes using three strands of dark gray floss.

🔘 Work the sweater in stem stitch using three strands of red floss. Work a row of small straight stitches along the lower edge using the same floss.

🔘 Work the pants in stem stitch using three strands of turquoise embroidery floss.

🔘 Work the boots in chain stitch using three strands of dark green embroidery floss.

🔘 Work the dog's leash in chain stitch using four strands of bright orange embroidery floss.

🔘 Outline the dog in chain stitch using three strands of dark gray embroidery floss. Work the dog markings in chain stitch using two strands of pale blue embroidery floss.

Make a French knot for the dog's eye using three strands of black embroidery floss. Make another French knot for the dog's nose using six strands of black floss.

Work the flower petals in lazy-daisy stitch using three strands of dusky pink embroidery floss. Make French knots for the flower centers using three strands of pale orange embroidery floss.

Work a series of straight stitches for the grass using three strands of lime green embroidery floss.

Work the center of the sun in chain stitch using three strands of bright yellow embroidery floss. Using the same floss, make straight stitches for the rays.

Use the red crayon to mark the cheeks.

stitch it!

This motif also looks great on a living-room cushion, a white cotton bag or a boy's craft apron.

The long and short of it

stitch it!

This design looks great on a tie for a dog lover, a small picture to hang by the hook for your dog's leash or even on a specially made dog's coat.

If you're a dog lover, chances are you can't resist a dachshund – the combination of slightly comical looks and lively personality are so appealing. They are also the ideal shape to embroider on anything long and thin! This little canine has been embroidered on a bookmark made from felt scraps.

Get stitching ...

Transfer the dog pattern on page 116 onto the cream felt.

Work the majority of the dog outline in stem stitch using three strands of medium brown embroidery floss. For the front paw, just showing under the sleeve of the sweater, work in backstitch using the same floss and for the top of the neck work a single straight stitch.

Make the sweater outline in chain stitch using three strands of lime green embroidery floss. Using the same floss, work a row of chain stitch at the bottom of the neck of the sweater. Again using the same floss, work a row of backstitch at the top of the lower rib section of the sweater and a single straight stitch at the top of the rib section of the sleeve. Work a series of single straight stitches to represent the ribbing at the lower, neck and sleeve edges of the sweater.

Work a single straight stitch for the mouth using three strands of red embroidery floss.

Make a French knot for the eye using three strands of dark gray embroidery floss.

Make a French knot for the nose using six strands of dark gray embroidery floss.

Lay the cream felt on the lime green felt. Work a row of running stitches around the cream felt using three strands of red floss.

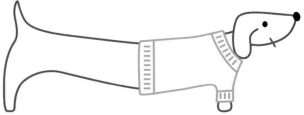

Blooming marvelous

Everyone loves flowers. So when it's chilly outside and the fields and meadows look bare, it's time to embroider your own. This design is shown on a small handmade pillow made from scraps of fabric. It works just as well on a plain ready-made pillow but if you want to make your own, see page 106.

Get stitching ...

Transfer the flowers pattern on page 116 onto your pillow or fabric panel. The width of the fabric panel should be greater than the height.

Work the stems of the three flowers in stem stitch using three strands of olive green embroidery floss. Using the same floss, work the leaves of the middle flower in stem stitch.

Make the leaves of the outer flowers in stem stitch using three strands of lime green embroidery floss,

adding a row of running stitch up the middle of the leaves of the tall flower.

Work the inner circle on the head of the tall flower in chain stitch using three strands of bright pink embroidery floss. Using the same floss, make the petals in lazy-daisy stitch. Work the outer circle of the flower in chain stitch using three strands of turquoise floss.

Work the circle on the head of the middle flower in chain stitch using three strands of royal blue embroidery floss. Make the petals in chain stitch using three strands of mauve embroidery floss.

Work the head of the small flower in chain stitch using three strands of deep pink embroidery floss. Make French knots for the stamens using three strands of pale orange embroidery floss.

Sew the buttons in the center of the tall and middle flowers.

If making your own cover, sew the pieces of the front of the pillow together and add the ribbon before completing the cover.

stitch it!

This design also looks great as a picture on a bedroom wall, on a bag or on lace-trimmed bed linen.

Knit one, purl one

Knitting is an ever-popular element in the world of crafts, so you're bound to know someone who could do with a brand-new box to hold all their projects. I made this simple fabric cover and lining for a shoe box from a piece of cotton twill and some leftover curtain fabric. You could just as easily use a ready-made fabric box, but if you want to make your own, see page 107.

Get stitching . . .

Transfer the pattern on page 117 onto your fabric or fabric box.

Work the ball of wool in backstitch using three strands of deep pink embroidery floss.

Work the knitting needles in stem stitch using three strands of medium green embroidery floss.

stitch it!

This motif is also suitable for a knitting bag, a craft apron or a felt book cover for a collection of knitting patterns.

Play

5

Jump for joy

High, low, medium, slow – jolly ol' pepper and away we go! Goodness knows where popular jumping-rope rhymes like this come from but they're a great reminder of how we girls used to spend our time. I made this apron from white cotton fabric and a simple homemade bias-binding trim. You could just as easily use a ready-made apron, but if you want to make your own, see page 108.

Get stitching ...

Transfer the jumping girl pattern on page 118 onto the apron or your pocket fabric.

Work the face and legs in stem stitch using two strands of pink embroidery floss. Using the same floss work the arms in stem stitch and the hands in scallop stitch. Again using the same floss, work two straight stitches, one over the other, for the nose.

Make the hair in backstitch using two strands of bright orange embroidery floss.

Work the mouth in backstitch using two strands of red embroidery floss.

Make French knots for the eyes using two strands of dark gray embroidery floss. Make the eyelashes in straight stitch using a single strand of dark gray floss.

Outline the dress in chain stitch using two strands of lime green embroidery floss. Work the dress collar and pocket in backstitch using the same thread. Again using the same floss, work a line of small running stitches for the dress pocket border.

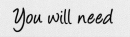

You will need

X Embroidery floss (thread) in the following colors:
   Pink for the face, nose, arms, hands and legs
   Bright orange for the hair
   Lime green for the dress
   Red for the shoes and mouth
   Mauve for the jump rope
   Bright yellow for the flowers
   Medium green for the grass and running-stitch border
   Dark gray for the eyes

X A red crayon for the cheeks

X Embroidery needle

X Embroidery scissors

X A ready-made apron or, if you want to make your own apron, fabrics, matching threads, a sewing machine, sewing scissors and an iron. If you are making your own apron, you will need a piece of fabric for the pocket measuring 8" x 9" (20 x 23 cm)

Stitches used

Straight stitch, running stitch, backstitch, stem stitch, satin stitch, chain stitch, lazy-daisy stitch, scallop stitch, French knot

Work the main part of the shoes in satin stitch using two strands of red embroidery floss. Using the same floss, work a backstitch border around the shoes and a single straight stitch for the bar of the shoes.

Make the jump rope in running stitch using three strands of mauve embroidery floss and work the rope handles in satin stitch using the same floss.

Work the flowers in lazy-daisy stitch using three strands of bright yellow floss.

Work the grass in straight stitch using three strands of medium-green embroidery floss.

If you are making your own apron, once the pocket has been stitched on the apron, work a running-stitch border using three strands of medium green floss.

stitch it!

This design also looks great on a pillow for a little girl's room, on a fabric storage box for toys or as a framed picture in the playroom.

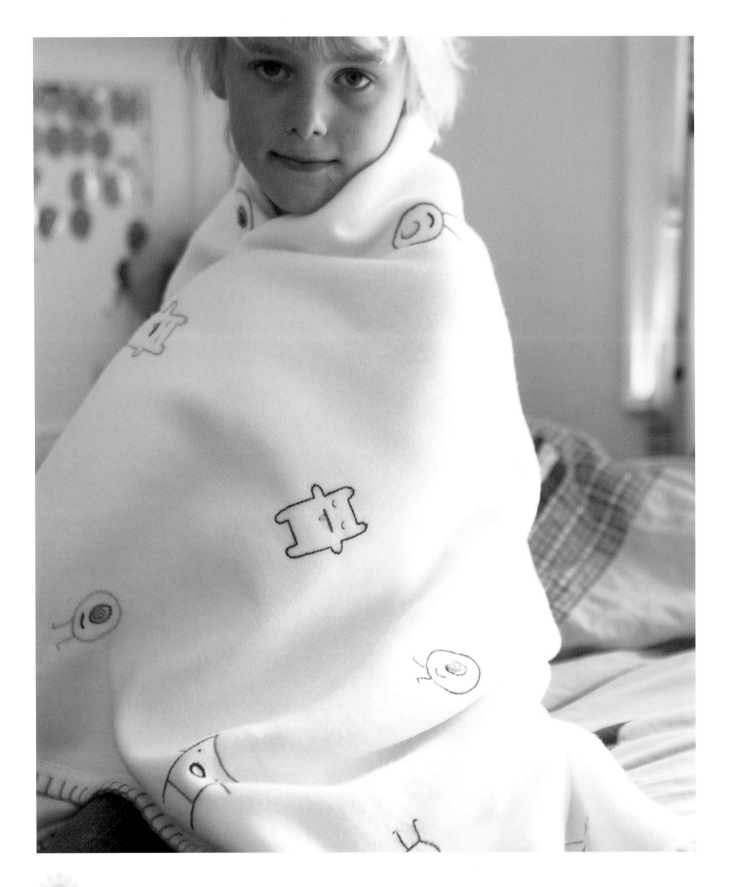

Three beasties

stitch it!

This design is also great on greeting cards and gift tags, on bed linen and on children's T-shirts.

Cute is good, but not all embroidery has to be sugary sweet. So what could be better than an embroidered monster – or three? These monsters have been stitched onto an inexpensive ready-made fleece throw.

Get stitching ...

Transfer the monster patterns on page 118 onto your fabric. Space them evenly over the throw at different angles to make them look scattered over the fleece.

There are three types of monsters: the round monster; the sleeping monster; the pointy-eared monster.

Outline all the monsters in stem stitch using three strands of embroidery floss, in a variety of colors (see box at left).

For the round monster, work the eye surround in stem stitch using three strands of embroidery floss in the color of your choice. Work the mouth in chain stitch using three strands of either red, deep or bright pink embroidery floss.

For the sleeping monster, work the eyes in backstitch using three strands of dark gray embroidery floss. Work the mouth in chain stitch using three strands of either red, deep or bright pink floss. Work a single scallop stitch for the tongue using three strands of medium pink embroidery floss.

For the pointy-eared monster, work the mouth in chain stitch using three strands of either red, deep or bright pink embroidery floss. Make a French knot for each eye using three strands of dark gray floss.

Sew the buttons for eyes onto the round monsters.

Work a blanket-stitch border around the entire throw using the olive green yarn.

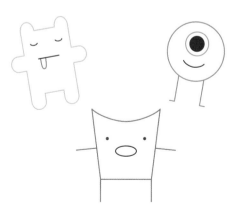

Big wheels keep on turning

Lots of little (and big) boys adore anything to do with cars and trucks, so why not make them some vehicle wall pockets for all their bits and pieces? These wall pockets are really simple to make.

Get stitching ...

Transfer the vehicle patterns on page 119 onto your pieces of felt. Remember to position your felt so that the height is greater than the width.

Outline the truck cab and bed in stem stitch using three strands of royal blue embroidery floss.

Outline the truck rack in stem stitch using three strands of turquoise embroidery floss. Using the same floss, work the markings in running stitch.

Work the truck window in stem stitch using three strands of medium gray embroidery floss.

Outline the car in stem stitch using three strands of red embroidery floss.

Work the car windows in stem stitch using three strands of dark gray embroidery floss.

Outline the main part of the camper in stem stitch using three strands of emerald embroidery floss. Work the tow hook in backstitch using the same floss.

Work the camper door and window outlines in stem stitch using three strands of bright orange embroidery floss. Work a row of running stitch for the trim using the same floss.

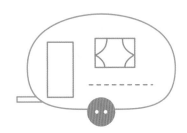

You will need

- X Embroidery floss (thread) in the following colors:
  Red for the car
  Dark gray for the car windows
  Royal blue for the truck cab and bed
  Turquoise for the truck rack
  Medium gray for the truck windows
  Emerald for the camper body
  Bright orange for the camper door, window and trim
  Mauve for the camper curtains
- X Two medium green buttons for the car
- X Two medium red buttons for the truck
- X One mauve button for the camper
- X Embroidery needle
- X Embroidery scissors
- X Six pieces of cream felt, each measuring 6¼" x 6¾ (16 x 17 cm), two for each pocket
- X Three 6" (15 cm) lengths of ribbon or tape, one for each pocket loop
- X Sewing thread to match your felt
- X Standard sewing needle or sewing machine
- X Sewing scissors

Stitches used

Running stitch, backstitch, stem stitch

• Work the curtains in backstitch using three strands of mauve embroidery floss.

• Fasten the red buttons on the truck, the green buttons on the car and the mauve button on the camper.

• Sew two pieces of felt together to make each pocket, leaving a seam allowance of ⅜" (1 cm). Turn down ⅜" (1 cm) at the top and stitch in place. Sew a loop of ribbon or tape on the back of each pocket. Hang them on nails, doorknobs or drawer handles.

stitch it!

These motifs are also fun on a T-shirt, on a simple cotton bag or on a bed cover for a child's room.

Big wheels keep on turning

Elephants on parade

Who doesn't adore elephants, particularly those floppy-eared, big-footed babies? Inspired by the beautifully decorated elephants that take part in Indian festivals, this cute pair is really simple to make. Once you've embroidered them, just sew around them, turn them right side out and get stuffing. I've made a mother and baby to start, but you could easily whip up a whole herd.

Get stitching . . .

- Transfer the elephant patterns on page 120 onto your fabric.

- *For the mother elephant,* outline the elephant in chain stitch using three strands of dark gray embroidery floss. Using the same floss, work the ear in running stitch.

- For the flower petals, make 6 lazy daisy stitches using six strands of purple embroidery floss. Make a French knot for the flower center using six strands of orange embroidery floss.

- For the toenails, work three scallop stitches using three strands of dusky pink floss.

- Make a French knot for the center of the eye using three strands of royal blue embroidery floss. Work seven straight stitches around the eye center using three strands of leaf green embroidery floss.

- *For the baby elephant,* work exactly as the mother elephant but use pale blue floss for the body and ear, red for the flower petals and yellow for the flower center.

- Trim around both your elephant embroideries leaving an inch or so (a few centimeters) of fabric all the way around.

- Place each embroidery face down on a second piece of fabric that is

You will need

- X Embroidery floss (thread) in the following colors:

  For the mother elephant
  Dark gray for the outline and ear
  Purple for the flower
  Orange for the flower center
  Royal blue for the center of the eye
  Leaf green for the outer eye
  Dusky pink for the toenails

  For the baby elephant
  Pale blue for the outline and ear
  Red for the flower
  Yellow for the flower center
  Royal blue for the center of the eye
  Leaf green for the outer eye
  Dusky pink for the toenails

- X Embroidery needle
- X Embroidery scissors
- X A small amount of midweight woven cotton fabric in off white
- X Matching sewing thread for your fabric
- X ½ oz (15 g) polyester toy stuffing (this will be sufficient to stuff both elephants)
- X Standard sewing needle or sewing machine
- X Sewing scissors
- X Iron

Stitches used

Straight stitch, running stitch, chain stitch, lazy-daisy stitch, scallop stitch, French knot

roughly the same size. Using matching thread, sew around the elephants about ¼" (5 to 7 mm) from the edge of the chain-stitched outline, leaving a gap between the legs for turning. You can use a sewing machine for this or sew by hand.

 Turn the elephants right side out through the gap and press lightly

using the iron. To get the seam to lie nicely around the edge of the elephant, try rolling it gently between your dampened thumb and forefinger before you press it.

 Stuff the elephant lightly; then sew the gap closed.

stitch it!

This design is perfect on a baby sleepsuit, on a small tote bag or on a pillow for a playroom – you could decorate the pillow with colorful ribbons or a pom-pom trim.

Dress

6

A little birdie told me

You will need

X Embroidery floss (thread) in the following colors:
Medium brown for the outline of the trunk and branches
Leaf green for the outline of the treetop
Bright red for the outline of the apples and the running-stitch border
Medium blue for the bird
Yellow for the bird's beak
Gray for the bird's eye

X Embroidery needle

X Embroidery scissors

X A child's white T-shirt

Stitches used

Straight stitch, running stitch, backstitch, chain stitch

Note

The main stitch used for this project is chain stitch. This is a very stable stitch and works well on stretchy knitted fabrics such as the cotton of this T-shirt. If you are embroidering this pattern on woven cotton, you could just as easily use stem stitch for the outline of the trunk, branches and treetop, if you prefer.

Sweet little birds used to be a mainstay of embroidery patterns in the 1950s and 1960s. So why did they all disappear? Now, thank goodness, cute has made a comeback – this time with just a hint of contemporary sophistication.

Get stitching ...

Transfer the bird in a tree pattern on page 122 onto your white T-shirt.

Outline the tree trunk and branches in chain stitch using three strands of medium brown embroidery floss.

Outline the treetop in chain stitch, using three strands of leaf green embroidery floss.

Outline each of the apples in chain stitch using three strands of red embroidery floss.

Work around the outline of the bird in chain stitch using two strands of medium blue embroidery floss and starting at one corner of the tail. Make a couple of straight stitches in the tail before fastening off.

Make the beak by working two small straight stitches in a V shape using two strands of yellow embroidery floss.

Work the eye in tiny backstitches, using a single strand of gray embroidery floss.

If you like, make a line of running stitches around the hem of the T-shirt using three strands of red embroidery floss.

stitch it!

This motif also works well on a plain white skirt, on bed linen or on a canvas tote bag.

Blowing in the wind

I love the sight of wash on a line, blowing in the breeze, and the smell of line-dried laundry. You could easily use a ready-made bag for this project, but if you want to make your own, cut two rectangles of linen, each measuring 14" x 17" (36 x 43 cm) and embroider the front before you sew the bag together.

Get stitching . . .

Transfer the pattern on page 121 onto one piece of fabric or onto the front of your bag.

Outline the shirt in stem stitch using three strands of leaf green embroidery floss. Using the same thread, work the collar in backstitch; then work the central line and cuff in running stitch.

Using three strands of red embroidery floss, make French knots for the buttons, winding the thread just once around the needle.

Outline the pants in stem stitch using three strands of turquoise embroidery floss. Work the hems of the pants in running stitch using two strands of the same floss.

Outline the dress in stem stitch using three strands of bright pink embroidery floss. Using the same floss, work the pocket in backstitch and the skirt trim in scallop stitch. Work the pocket trim in running stitch using two strands of the same floss.

Make the clothesline in running stitch using three strands of dark gray floss.

Make single straight stitches for the clothespins using three strands of terracotta embroidery floss.

Sew on the flowers or work some lazy-daisy stitches to make flowers in your chosen colors. If using a ready-made bag, you have now finished.

If you're making your own bag, sew the two main pieces together at the sides and bottom and double hem the top edge. The drawstring casing is made from a 1¼" x 27½" (3 x 70 cm) strip of printed cotton. Press down ¾" (1.5 cm) around all the edges of the strip. Now sew the strip in place about 1½" (4 cm) down from the top so that the two short edges form a space on the right-hand side for the drawstring, which should be about 39" (1 m) long. Thread the drawstring through the casing.

stitch it!

Use this design on a pillow, as a simple framed picture for the kitchen or on a clothespin bag.

Dress

Never mind the weather

Sneakers are comfy and cool for a long, hot summer. And while plain ones have their place, if you want something a little special, try adding your own motifs. It's not half as difficult as it looks – simple, small motifs like these work best.

Get stitching . . .

Transfer the weather patterns on page 121 onto the sneakers.

Outline the cloud in chain stitch using three strands of blue-gray embroidery floss. Work the rain in running stitch using two strands of pale gray floss.

Outline the sun in chain stitch using three strands of bright yellow embroidery floss. Using the same floss, work a series of straight stitches for the rays.

Work both mouths in backstitch using three strands of crimson embroidery floss.

Make French knots for the eyes of the cloud and sun using three strands of dark gray embroidery floss.

Note

It is fairly easy to embroider sneakers, particularly if you stuff them with tissue paper. You can secure your thread at the beginning of your work by making a knot in the normal way. However, it is a bit harder to secure your thread when you have finished your stitching. Either make a couple of tiny stitches on the front of your work, and then take your thread to the inside and trim, or take your thread to the inside and dab it with a spot of fabric glue.

stitch it!

This design also looks great on pants pockets, little felt wall pockets or around the border of a tablecloth for an outdoor table.

A rose is a rose is a rose

A red rose is shorthand for love and is one of the best-known motifs ever. Although it's been around for so long, I couldn't possibly leave it out of this collection. So here is my very own stitched rose, shown on a ready-made bag.

Get stitching . . .

- Transfer the rose pattern on page 122 onto your bag.

- Work the main part of the rose in chain stitch using three strands of deep pink embroidery floss.

- Make French knots for the stamens using three strands of pale orange embroidery floss.

- Work the stem and leaf outlines in stem stitch using three strands of olive green floss. Using the same floss, work the veins of the leaves in running stitch.

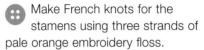

stitch it!

A rose motif looks great on a greeting card for a loved one or on the pocket of your favorite jeans. It also adds a touch of romance to your bed linen.

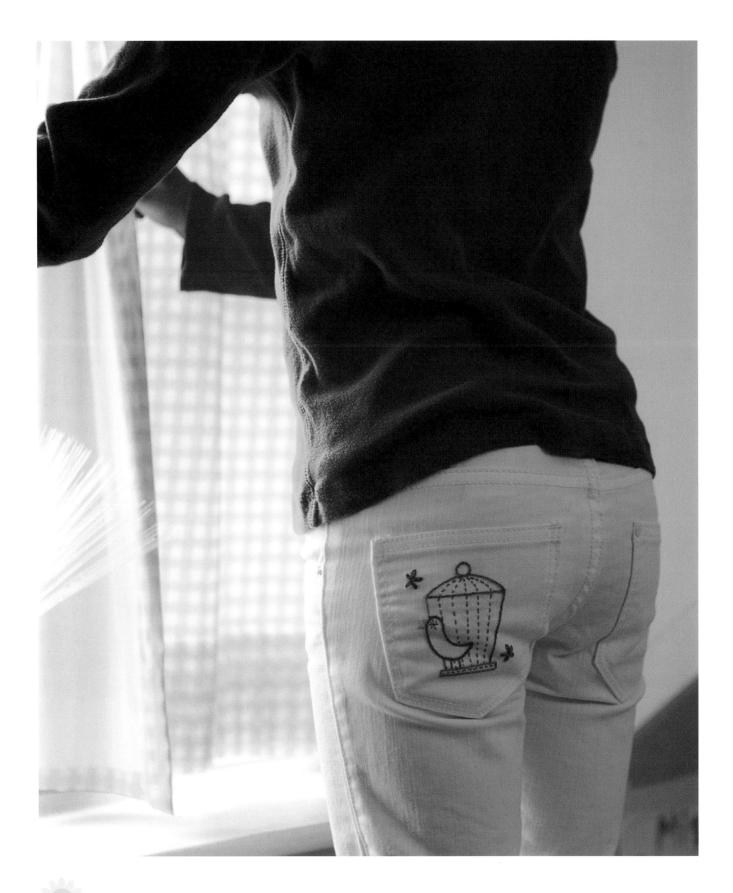

Chirpy chirpy cheep cheep

stitch it!

This birdie motif is also great on a greeting card, on a felt wall pocket or as a tiny framed picture.

These days we know that birds should really be flying free and not cooped up in a cage – even a pretty Victorian one. So this little fellow, hiding on the pocket of a pair of jeans, is singing to celebrate his freedom!

Get stitching . . .

Transfer the pattern on page 122 onto the pocket of the jeans.

Work the bird in chain stitch using three strands of bright pink embroidery floss.

For the bird's legs work two single straight stitches using three strands of bright orange embroidery floss.

Work two single straight stitches for the beak using six strands of pale orange embroidery floss.

Make a French knot for the eye using three strands of dark gray embroidery floss, remembering to wind the thread just once around the needle instead of the usual twice. Work tiny straight stitches around the eye using a single strand of the same color floss.

Outline the cage in stem stitch using three strands of denim blue embroidery floss. Using the same floss, work the cage bars and trim along the base of the cage in running stitch. Work the cage loop in chain stitch, again using the same floss.

Make the flowers in lazy-daisy stitch using three strands of mauve embroidery floss.

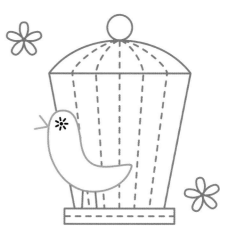

Bath

7

A whale of a time

A whale leaping out of the ocean is a magnificent sight. In all honesty, this whale is unlikely to be doing much leaping, but he looks perfect on this ready-made shower cap and would make a jolly addition to many other bathroom items.

Get stitching ...

- Transfer the whale pattern on page 124 onto your shower cap.

- Outline the whale in chain stitch using three strands of bright blue embroidery floss. Work the mouth in backstitch using three strands of the same floss.

- Work the water spout in running stitch using four strands of pale gray floss.

- Make a French knot for the eye using three strands of dark gray embroidery floss. Using the same floss, work small straight stitches around the eye.

stitch it!
This whale looks great on bathroom towels, on a pajama pocket or on a fabric lampshade for a child's bedroom.

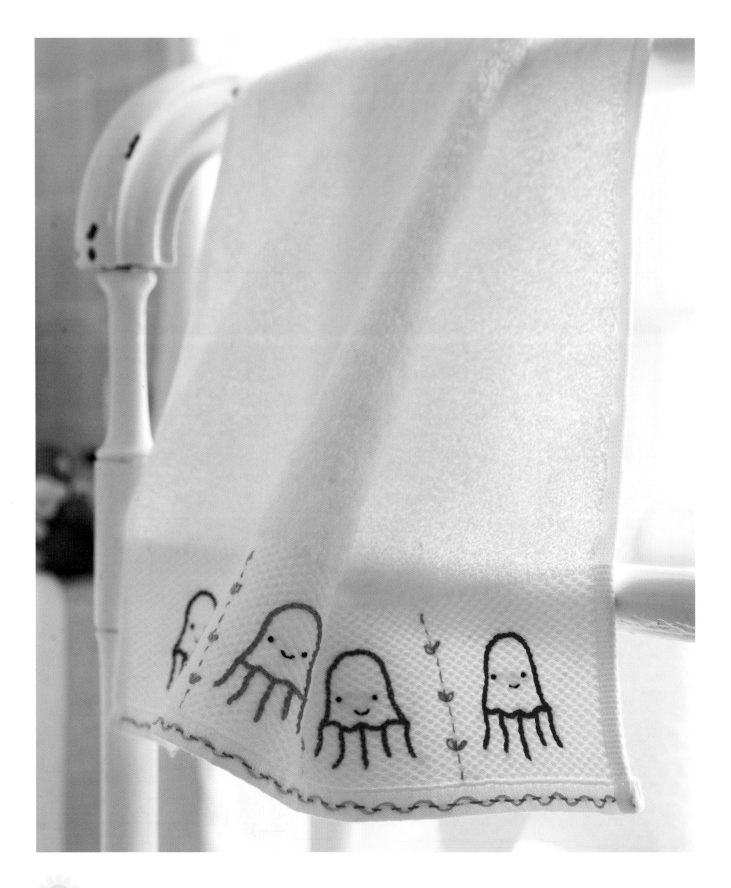

Under the sea

Plain white towels, beloved of hotels everywhere, are . . . well, a bit boring, actually. But who could resist a towel with these delightful little jellyfish? I've stitched these little fellows in shades of pink and red, but you can sew them in any colors you like to match your bathroom.

You will need

X Embroidery floss (thread) in the following colors:
Deep pink, bright pink, orange, dusky pink and red for the jellyfish
Purple for the mouths
Dark gray for the eyes
Leaf green for the seaweed
Medium blue and pale blue for the threaded running-stitch border

X Embroidery needle

X Embroidery scissors

X A plain white towel with a woven border at least 2¾" (7 cm) deep

Stitches used

Running stitch, threaded running stitch, backstitch, chain stitch, lazy-daisy stitch, French knot

Get stitching . . .

Transfer the jellyfish and seaweed pattern on page 124 onto your towel. You will need to make sure your jellyfish and seaweed are evenly spaced across the border of your towel.

Work the body and legs of each jellyfish in chain stitch using three strands of embroidery floss in deep pink, bright pink, orange, dusky pink or red.

Work the mouths in backstitch using three strands of purple embroidery floss.

Make French knots for the eyes using three strands of dark gray embroidery floss.

Work a vertical row of running stitch for the seaweed using three strands of leaf green floss. Work the leaves in lazy-daisy stitch.

Make a row of running stitch along the edge of the towel using three strands of medium blue embroidery floss. Then weave three strands of pale blue embroidery floss through these stitches.

stitch it!

This design looks great on a shower cap, on a bathroom curtain or on a cotton bathrobe.

Squeaky clean

Don't you just love that time of day when you can climb into a hot bath and soak all your worries away? If you do, then immortalize the moment in a picture stitched on white cotton fabric, stretched over an inexpensive artist's canvas and stapled in place.

Get stitching ...

- Transfer the pattern on page 123 onto your fabric.

- Work the bath and feet in stem stitch using three strands of purple embroidery floss. Using the same floss, work a couple of small straight stitches on the feet of the bath to represent the claws.

- Work the shower and main part of the tap in dark gray stem stitch. Using the same floss, work the handle of the tap in backstitch.

- Work the water spray in running stitch using three strands of pale blue floss. Using the same floss, work the bubbles in backstitch.

- Outline the face and arms in stem stitch using three strands of pink embroidery floss. Using the same floss, work the hand in scallop stitch and a single straight stitch for the nose.

- Work the mouth in backstitch using three strands of crimson embroidery floss.

- Work the hair in backstitch using three strands of terracotta embroidery floss.

- Make French knots for the girl's eyes using three strands of dark gray embroidery floss. Work small straight stitches for the eyelashes using two strands of the same floss.

- Outline the duck and the wing in chain stitch using two strands of bright yellow floss. Work two straight stitches for the bill using three strands of bright orange floss.

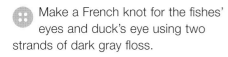 Work the fish in chain stitch using two strands each of the three green colors.

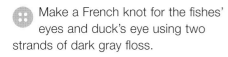 Make a French knot for the fishes' eyes and duck's eye using two strands of dark gray floss.

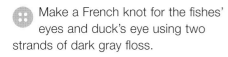 Work the sponge in chain stitch using three strands of mint green floss. Using the same floss, make French knots for the holes.

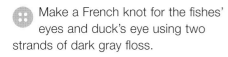 Make the curtains in stem stitch using three strands of bright pink embroidery floss. Using the same floss, add a row of backstitches at the center of each curtain and two straight stitches along the hem of each curtain.

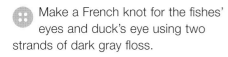 Work the top and bottom of the window in stem stitch using three strands of lime green embroidery floss. Make the windowpanes in running stitch using the same floss.

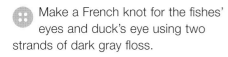 Use the red crayon for the cheeks.

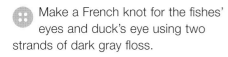 Iron the fabric; then stretch it over the artist's frame and staple it in place using the staple gun.

stitch it!

This design is fun on a drawstring bag for storing bath toys, a fabric-covered storage box or on a cushion for a bathroom stool.

Sail away with me

stitch it!

This nautical motif also looks great on a drawstring bag for a boy's bedroom, a greeting card or a T-shirt.

Sailboats remind me of childhood holidays by the sea. They're cheerful, mysterious and romantic, all at the same time, so it's no wonder that they're such a popular motif in bathrooms around the world. I've used a simple handmade doorstop for the sailboat here. For instructions on how to make one, see page 109.

Get stitching . . .

Transfer the pattern on page 124 onto one of the large surfaces of your doorstop. If you are making your own doorstop, embroider it before you sew it together.

Work the sails in stem stitch using three strands of denim blue embroidery floss.

Work the mast in stem stitch using three strands of medium gray embroidery floss.

Outline the boat in chain stitch using three strands of red floss. Make the stripe in running stitch using three strands of denim-blue embroidery floss.

Work the flag in satin stitch using three strands of red embroidery floss. Outline the flag in small backstitches using a single strand of the same color.

Make the gulls in backstitch, using three strands of medium gray embroidery floss.

Make the cloud in chain stitch, using three strands of pale blue embroidery floss.

Stitch the blue rickrack around the bottom of the doorstop. If you are making your own doorstop, add the rickrack once you have sewn the sides of the doorstop together but before you have stuffed the doorstop or sewn the base.

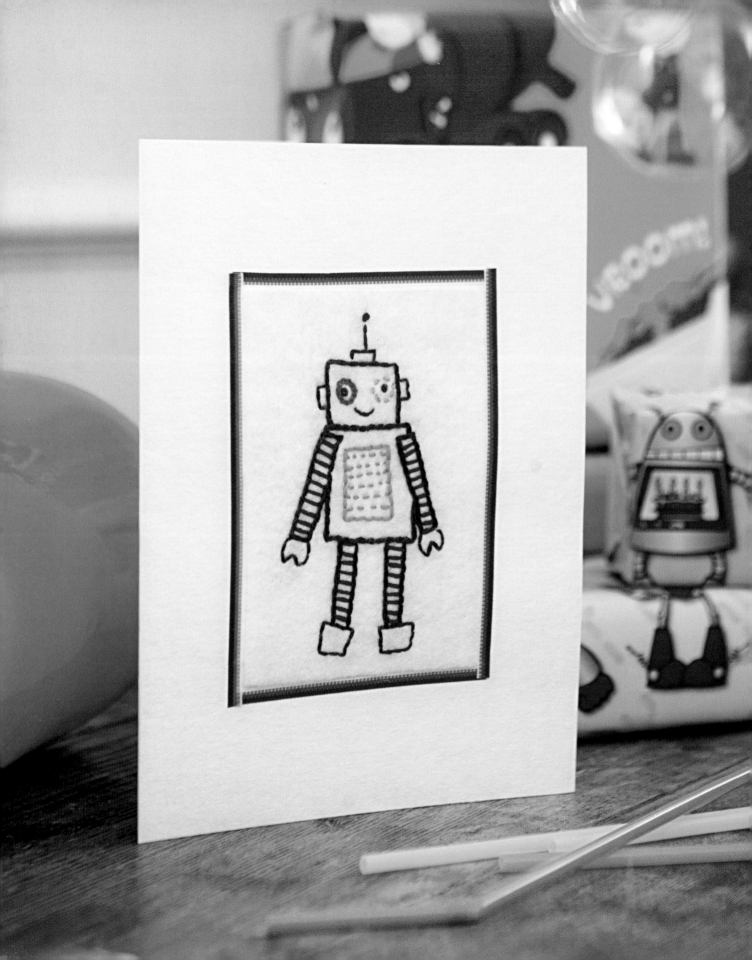

Celebrate

8

Away with the fairies

Dreamy and mysterious, delicate and floaty – it's no wonder so many little girls (and some bigger ones too) want to look like fairies. If you know anyone who's crazy about the make-believe world of fairies, they'll love this little darling who has been embroidered on felt and glued to a ready-made blank card.

Get stitching . . .

Transfer the fairy pattern on page 125 onto your piece of felt.

Work the face, legs and arms in stem stitch using three strands of light brown embroidery floss. Using the same floss, work the hands in scallop stitch. Work a single straight stitch for the nose, again using the same floss.

Make the hair in backstitch using three strands of dark brown embroidery floss.

Make two French knots for the eyes using three strands of dark gray embroidery floss. Using a single strand of the same floss, make three short straight stitches for the eyelashes.

Work the mouth in backstitch using three strands of red embroidery floss.

Work the outline of the dress in chain stitch using three strands of lime green floss. Using the same floss, work the base of the bodice in backstitch. Using two strands of the same floss, work the gather lines in running stitch.

Make two French knots for the buttons using three strands of deep pink floss, winding the thread just once around the needle. Work a row of running stitches across the hem of the dress using two strands of pale pink floss.

Make the wings in running stitch, using three strands of deep pink embroidery floss.

Work the shoes in satin stitch using three strands of deep pink embroidery floss. Using the same floss, make a cross at the top of each shoe for the ribbons.

Work the wand in backstitch, using three strands of bright yellow embroidery floss. Using the same floss, add a star stitch at the top to complete the wand.

Color the cheeks with the pink crayon.

Using fabric glue, adhere the felt panel to the blank card and glue the narrow lace around the border.

stitch it!

This fairy looks magical on a bag to hold ballet shoes, on a little girl's T-shirt or as a small picture for a bedroom.

Cool robot

You will need

Robots seem to have been around for ages and are a favorite motif of small boys. Try stitching your own prototype for a boy in your life. This robot has been embroidered on felt and glued to a ready-made blank card.

Get stitching . . .

- Transfer the robot pattern on page 125 onto your piece of felt.

- Outline the head, torso, arms and legs in stem stitch using three strands of dark gray embroidery floss. Using the same floss, work the ears, very top of the head, hands and feet using backstitch.

- Work the mouth in backstitch, using three strands of purple embroidery floss. Using the same floss, make two French knots for the centers of the eyes. Work the outer part of the robot's right eye in chain stitch, using two strands of royal blue floss. Work the outer part of the robot's left eye in running stitch using three strands of lime green embroidery floss.

- Make the stripes along the arms and legs in straight stitch using three strands of red embroidery floss. Using the same floss, make the antenna at the top of the head in backstitch, with a French knot to represent the antenna tip.

- Outline the center panel in backstitch using three strands of turquoise floss. Using the same floss, work the lines on the panel in running stitch.

- Using fabric glue, adhere the felt panel to the blank card. Use the narrow self-adhesive ribbon to make a border.

You will need

X **Embroidery floss (thread)** in the following colors:
Dark gray for the main outline
Red for the stripes and antenna
Turquoise for the central panel
Purple for the eyes and mouth
Royal blue for the outline of the robot's right eye
Lime green for the outline of the robot's left eye

X **Embroidery needle**

X **Embroidery scissors**

X **A piece of white felt** measuring 3¼" x 4¾" (8 x 12 cm)

X **A piece of narrow self-adhesive ribbon** for the border, measuring approximately 12" (30 cm)

X **A blank card** 6" x 8¼" (15 x 21 cm)

X **Fabric glue**

Stitches used

Straight stitch, running stitch, backstitch, stem stitch, chain stitch, French knot

stitch it!

This design looks great made into a small stuffed toy, on a T-shirt or on children's place mats.

Up the garden path

Snail worship is a little-known activity relegated to a dedicated few. But who could resist the endearing shelled creature in this picture? If you love wildlife, please try stitching the snail as well as the adorable aphid-gobbling ladybug! These gift tags are embroidered on scraps of felt that are adhered to ready-made cardboard luggage labels.

Get stitching . . .

 Transfer the snail and ladybug patterns on page 126 onto your pieces of felt.

 For the snail, work the body in stem stitch using three strands of orange embroidery floss. Using the same floss work the antennae in backstitch with French knots at the end.

 Work the shell in stem stitch using three strands of turquoise embroidery floss. Using the same floss, work the coil in running stitch.

 Make French knots for the snail's eyes using two strands of dark gray embroidery floss, remembering to wind the thread just once around the needle instead of the usual twice. Using the same floss, work the mouth in backstitch.

 Make several single straight stitches for the grass using three strands of lime green embroidery floss.

 Make the border in running stitch using three strands of medium pink embroidery floss.

 For the ladybug, work the body in chain stitch using three strands of red floss. Make French knots for the spots using three strands of black floss.

 Work the face in stem stitch using two strands of dark gray embroidery floss. Using the same floss, make the two antennae in backstitch.

 Work the legs in straight stitch using three strands of black embroidery floss.

Make French knots for the eyes using two strands of dark gray embroidery floss. Work the mouth in backstitch using two strands of red embroidery floss.

Do several single straight stitches for the grass using three strands of medium green embroidery floss.

Work the border in running stitch using three strands of denim blue embroidery floss.

Trim the embroidered scraps and use fabric glue to adhere them to the luggage labels.

stitch it!

These cute little creatures also look great on baby clothes, as a border on a curtain or on decor for a garden room or summerhouse.

Love is like a butterfly

stitch it!

A butterfly motif is fun on children's clothes, felt wall pockets for a girl's bedroom or as little stuffed creatures strung together to form a mobile.

Nothing reminds me more that it's summer than watching a butterfly flitting from flower to flower. Sadly, this experience can't last forever, so I whipped up a summery decoration to keep the memories alive. The butterflies are embroidered on felt pennants, and then sewn together on a strip of bias binding.

Get stitching . . .

Cut the felt squares into eight triangles or pennants, each measuring 6" (15 cm) across the base and 7" (18 cm) from the midpoint of the base to the tip. It is a good idea to make a template from cardboard, which you can then simply trace around.

Transfer the butterfly pattern on page 126 onto your pennants so that each butterfly is situated in the same place on the triangle.

Work the bodies and antennae in stem stitch using three strands of dark gray embroidery floss. Make French knots for the eyes using the same floss, remembering to wind the floss just once round the needle instead of the usual twice. Work the mouth in backstitch, again using the same floss.

Make the wings in chain stitch, using three strands of one of the different brightly colored floss for each butterfly.

Sew buttons to the top part of the wings for each of the butterflies, using contrasting colored thread.

Fold the bias binding in half and baste the pennants evenly along the length of the binding, leaving a long enough tail at either end to fasten the pennant strand. Machine or hand stitch along the edges of the binding, including the tails.

Make your own stuff to stitch

The following are basic instructions on how to make some of the items featured in this book. While a sewing machine is not absolutely essential, your work will be stronger and have a more professional finish if you use one.

All seam allowances are ⅜" (1 cm). All measurements are given in imperial and then in metric figures. To make life easy for yourself, stick to one set of measurements or the other; don't mix the two or the result may be less than satisfactory!

Place mat

See page 22 and use the photo as a guide.

The finished mat is approximately 9" x 12½" (22 x 29 cm).

Once you have embroidered the main panel of the mat, sew the two short fabric strips to the short sides of the mat and press the seam allowances open. Then sew the two long strips across the top and bottom and press the seam allowances open.

Iron the interfacing onto the backing fabric. Lay the front and back of the mat right sides together and sew around the edge, leaving a gap at the middle of the lower edge for turning.

Clip the corners, turn the mat right side out and press. Top stitch around the outside of the mat about ¼" (5 mm) from the outside edge.

You will need
(for one mat)

X A piece of fabric for the main panel measuring 6¼" x 9" (16 x 23 cm)

X Two strips of contrasting fabric measuring 2½" x 6¼" (6 x 16 cm)

X Two strips of the same contrasting fabric measuring 2½" x 12¼" (6 x 31 cm)

X A piece of fabric for the back measuring 9½" x 12¼" (24 x 31 cm)

X A piece of iron-on interfacing measuring 9½" x 12¼" (24 x 31 cm)

Cotton bag

See page 49 and use the photo as a guide.

The finished bag (excluding handles) is approximately 10" (25 cm) square.

For the binding, cut 2½"-wide (6 cm) strips of fabric on the bias. You will need two 8¼"-long (21 cm) strips for the bag top and two 22"-long (56 cm) strips for the sides and handles. Sew strips together diagonally if you do not have sufficient fabric to cut single lengths.

Follow the diagram below to make your bag template, then cut out two identical pieces of fabric for the front and back of the bag.

Once you have embroidered the bag front, sew the darts at the bottom of the two bag pieces.

To prepare the binding, fold the long raw edges of the strips to the center and press. Then fold the strips in half and press again. Baste the short strips across the tops of the bag pieces and stitch them in place. Then baste and stitch the long pieces in place to form the sides and handles. Now sew the front and back of the bag together and trim the seam allowances.

You will need

X Two rectangles of cotton fabric, each measuring about 12½" (32 cm) square

X Contrasting fabric to make the binding

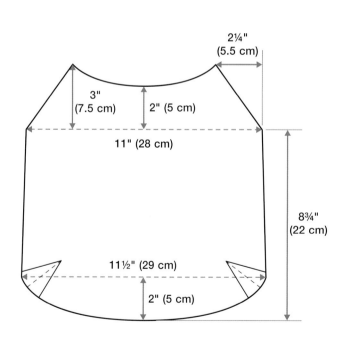

2¼" (5.5 cm)

3" (7.5 cm)

2" (5 cm)

11" (28 cm)

8¾" (22 cm)

11½" (29 cm)

2" (5 cm)

Pillow cover

See page 59 and use the photo as a guide.

The pillow cover is designed to fit a 12" (30 cm) square pillow. The cover is slightly smaller so that the pillow looks plump.

After embroidering the panel, sew it to the side panel and press the seam allowances open. Then sew this piece to the lower panel and press the seam allowances open. Stitch the trim in place.

For the back of the pillow, hem one of the long sides of each of the two back pieces. Sew them to the front of the pillow cover so that the hemmed side of the top back piece overlaps the lower back piece. Clip the corners and turn right side out.

Stitch the snap at the center of the overlapped pieces and sew the button in the center of the lower edge of the top flap, over the snap.

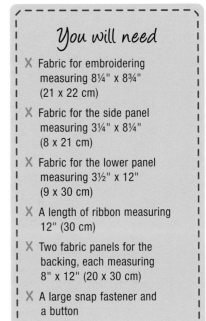

You will need

X Fabric for embroidering measuring 8¼" x 8¾" (21 x 22 cm)

X Fabric for the side panel measuring 3¼" x 8¼" (8 x 21 cm)

X Fabric for the lower panel measuring 3½" x 12" (9 x 30 cm)

X A length of ribbon measuring 12" (30 cm)

X Two fabric panels for the backing, each measuring 8" x 12" (20 x 30 cm)

X A large snap fastener and a button

Fabric-lined knitting box

You will need

✕ Fabric for the outer and inner covers – exactly how much you need depends on the dimensions of your box

See page 60 and use the photo as a guide.

These details explain how to make a fabric cover for a box such as a large shoebox.

⊞ Loosely measure the base and sides of your box and cut out a shape from your outer fabric and lining fabric, as shown below.

⊞ Sew the four side seams of the outer cover and lining to form two box shapes. Double-hem around the top of the lining fabric (you do not have to hem the fabric for the outer part of the box).

⊞ Once you have embroidered the outer cover, place it over the box and tuck the top edge into the box. Then position the lining and pull the top part of the lining up over the edges of the box. You may find it useful to position the cover on the box before you start your embroidery in order to work out where to place the motif.

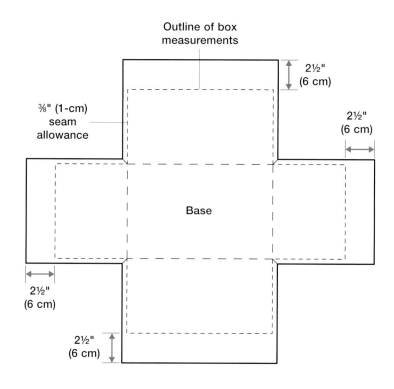

Outline of box measurements

2½" (6 cm)

⅜" (1-cm) seam allowance

2½" (6 cm)

Base

2½" (6 cm)

2½" (6 cm)

Child's apron

See page 65 and use the photo as a guide.

The apron will fit a child approximately 6 to 10 years of age.

○ Cut enough 1¾"-wide (4.5 cm) strips of fabric on the bias to equal a strip measuring 2 yards (2 m) in length for the waist ties, upper sides and head loop, and a strip measuring 1¼ yards (1.25 m) in length for the lower sides and hem. Sew strips together diagonally if you do not have sufficient fabric to cut single lengths.

○ Cut the main piece for the apron using the guidelines below.

○ Once you have embroidered and stitched the pocket, prepare the binding. Fold the long raw edges of the strips to the center and press. Then fold the strips in half and press again.

○ Baste and stitch the binding around the lower sides and bottom first; then baste and stitch the binding around the sides and top, allowing 14" (35 cm) of binding to form the head loop. Stitch the binding together without the apron fabric to form the waist ties.

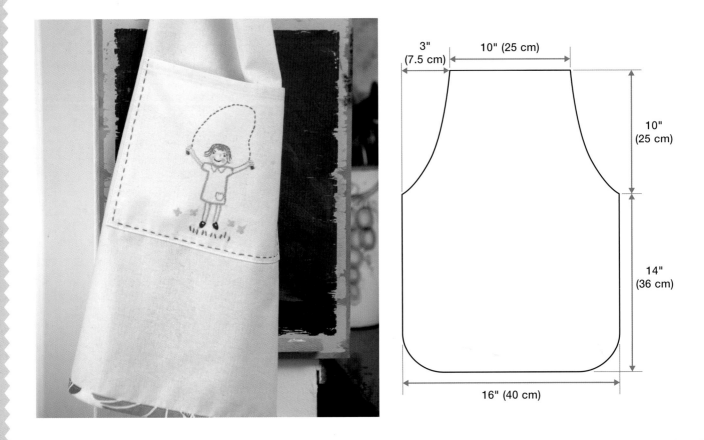

Doorstop

See page 92 and use the photo as a guide.

- Cut out the doorstop and handle shapes as shown below.

- Make the handle of the doorstop by folding up ⅜" (1 cm) on the long lower edge and 1¼" (3 cm) at the top edge of the fabric; then fold along the central line and top stitch along both sides.

- Fasten the handle to the center top of the doorstop using 1" (2.5 cm) stitched squares with a diagonal cross.

- Once you have embroidered the doorstop, sew it into a brick shape, leaving a gap on one of the lower edges so that you can stuff it. Stuff the doorstop; then stitch the opening closed.

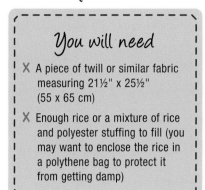

7" (18 cm)

1¼" (3 x 3 cm)

4⅛" (10 cm)

⅜" (1 cm)

Handle

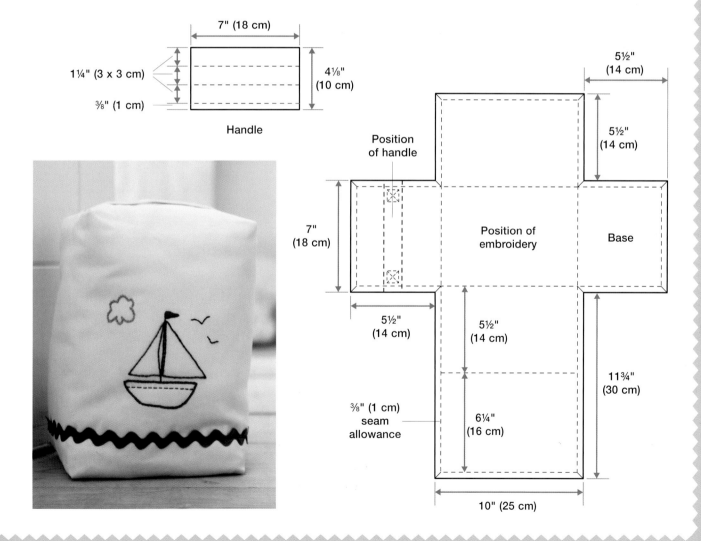

Position of handle

5½" (14 cm)

5½" (14 cm)

7" (18 cm)

Position of embroidery

Base

5½" (14 cm)

5½" (14 cm)

11¾" (30 cm)

⅜" (1 cm) seam allowance

6¼" (16 cm)

10" (25 cm)

The patterns

Café society
pages 20 and 21

A nice cup of tea
pages 22 and 23

Let them eat cake
pages 24 and 25

Kitchen sink drama
pages 26 and 27

Sweetest little baby face
pages 28 and 29

Dream a little dream
pages 38 and 39

Do the funky chicken
pages 30 and 31

Give me the moonlight
pages 36 and 37

The cat's whiskers
pages 34 and 35

Bunny hugs
pages 40 and 41

Home sweet home
pages 44 and 45

Pen friends
pages 46 and 47

Wise old owl
pages 48 and 49

Ring my bell
pages 50 and 51

Blooming marvelous
pages 58 and 59

The long and short of it
pages 56 and 57

The perfect pooch
pages 54 and 55

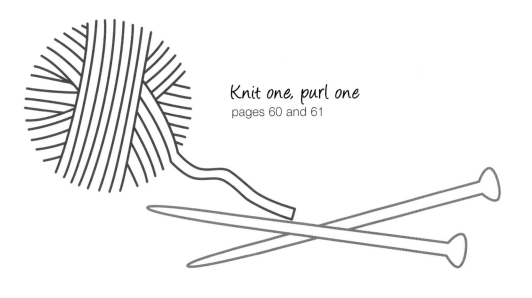

Knit one, purl one
pages 60 and 61

Jump for joy
pages 64 and 65

Three beasties
pages 66 and 67

Big wheels keep on turning
pages 68 and 69

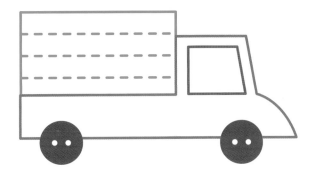

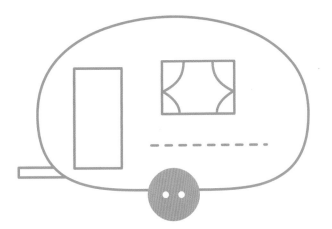

Elephants on parade
pages 70 and 71

Blowing in the wind
pages 76 and 77

Never mind the weather
pages 78 and 79

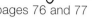

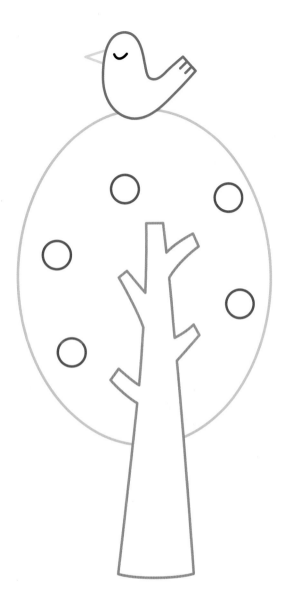

A rose is a rose is a rose
pages 80 and 81

A little birdie told me
pages 74 and 75

Chirpy chirpy cheep cheep
pages 82 and 83

 **122**   The patterns

Squeaky clean
pages 90 and 91

Under the sea
pages 88 and 89

A whale of a time
pages 86 and 87

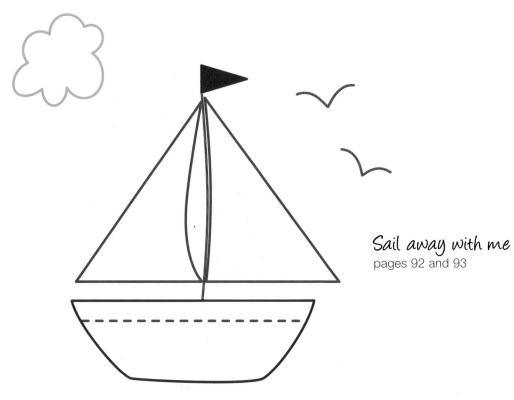

Sail away with me
pages 92 and 93

Away with the fairies
pages 96 and 97

Cool robot
pages 98 and 99

Up the garden path
pages 100 and 101

Love is like a butterfly
pages 102 and 103

Index

Acknowledgments

The projects in this book have been sewn using DMC embroidery floss.
www.dmc.com

With thanks to Paddy and David Goble and Roger and Louis Dromard for their enthusiasm and patience.